EXPLORE OUTER SPACE

SATURN

by Ruth Owen

WINDMILL
BOOKS

New York

Published in 2014 by Windmill Books, An Imprint of Rosen Publishing
29 East 21st Street, New York, NY 10010

Produced for Windmill by Ruby Tuesday Books Ltd
Editor for Ruby Tuesday Books Ltd: Mark J. Sachner
US Editor: Joshua Shadowens
Designer: Trudi Webb
Consultant: Kevin Yates, Fellow of the Royal Astronomical Society

Library of Congress Cataloging-in-Publication Data

Owen, Ruth, 1967–
 Saturn / by Ruth Owen.
    pages cm. — (Explore outer space)
 ISBN 978-1-61533-727-9 — ISBN 978-1-61533-771-2 (pbk.) —
 ISBN 978-1-61533-772-9
 1. Saturn (Planet)—Juvenile literature. 2. Saturn (Planet)—Exploration—Juvenile literature.
3. Saturn (Planet)—Ring system—Juvenile literature. 4. Cassini (Spacecraft)—Juvenile
literature. I. Title. II. Series: Owen, Ruth, 1967– Explore outer space.
 QB671.O935 2014
 523.46—dc23
                                        2013013967

Manufactured in the United States of America

CPSIA Compliance Information: Batch #BS13WM: For Further Information contact Windmill Books, New York, New York at 1-866-478-0556

CONTENTS

THE RINGED WONDER

Saturn is the sixth-farthest **planet** from the Sun. As it **orbits** the Sun, it is an average distance of nearly 900 million miles (1.4 billion km) from the **star** at the center of our **solar system**. That's about nine and a half times farther from the Sun than our planet.

Saturn is the second-largest planet in the solar system. If Earth were the size of a marble, huge Saturn would be just a little larger than a soccer ball. This enormous planet is probably known best for the thousands of beautiful rings, made of ice, dust, and rock, that encircle it.

Unlike the planet that we call home, Saturn is not a ball of rock. Instead, it is a massive ball of hydrogen and helium gas. Along with Jupiter, Uranus, and Neptune, Saturn is known as a gas giant because it is a giant ball of gases and liquids!

That's Out of This World!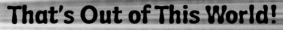

Like Mercury, Venus, Mars, and Jupiter, Saturn is visible in the night sky with the naked eye. The ancient Romans observed these planets and named them after their gods. Saturn is named for the Roman god of agriculture.

Saturn's rings

Earth

The sizes of Saturn and Earth are shown to scale here. In real life, of course, the planets are not this close together. In fact, as it orbits the Sun, Saturn is an average distance from Earth of about 900 million miles (1.4 billion km).

A Solar System is Born

About five billion years ago, the Sun, Mercury, Venus, Earth, Mars, Jupiter, Saturn, Uranus, and Neptune did not exist.

The chemical ingredients that created the Sun, the planets, and everything else in the solar system, were floating in a vast cloud of gas and dust called a **nebula**.

Over millions of years, part of the cloud began to collapse on itself, forming a massive rotating sphere, or ball. A disk formed around this sphere from the remaining gas and dust. As the material in the sphere became pressed together by **gravity**, pressure built up and the temperature in the sphere's core rose to around 18 million °F (10 million°C). Eventually, the heat and pressure became so great that the sphere ignited, and became a star. This new star was our Sun.

Gas and dust continued to spin in a disk around the newly formed star. Over time, this gas and dust clumped together to form planets, **dwarf planets**, **moons**, **asteroids**, and every other object in the solar system.

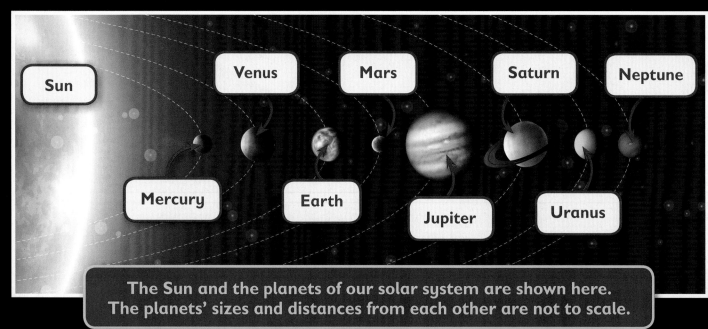

The Sun and the planets of our solar system are shown here.
The planets' sizes and distances from each other are not to scale.

That's Out of This World!

Mercury, Venus, Earth, and Mars have solid rocky surfaces. These four planets formed closest to the Sun. Jupiter, Saturn, Uranus, and Neptune, the furthest planets from the Sun, do not have solid surfaces. These huge planets are made mostly of gas and are known as the gas giants.

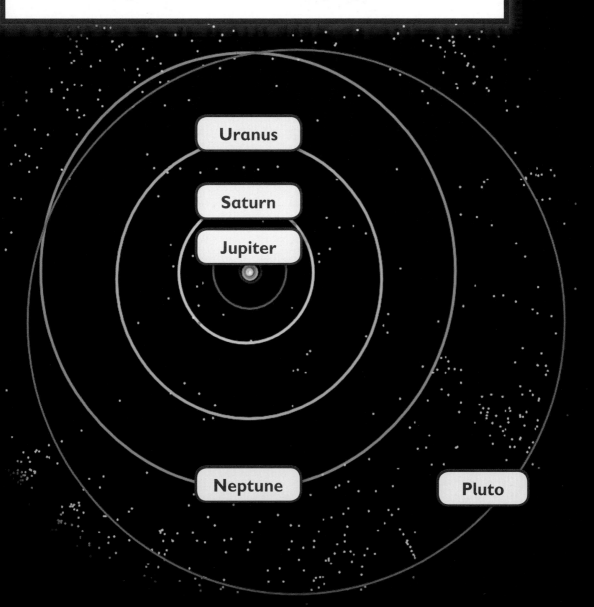

Uranus

Saturn

Jupiter

Neptune

Pluto

This diagram shows the orbits (the colored circles) of Jupiter, Saturn, Uranus, and Neptune, which are the four planets that are furthest from the Sun. The orbit of Pluto, which is a dwarf planet, is also shown.

SATURN'S YEARS AND DAYS

Like all the objects in the solar system, Saturn is orbiting the Sun. As it travels through space, Saturn is moving at about 21,500 miles per hour (34,600 km/h).

Our planet orbits the Sun once every 365 days, a time period we call a year. Saturn is so far from the Sun, however, that it takes 10,756 days for the planet to make one full orbit. This means that a year on Saturn lasts just over 29 Earth years! During a single orbit of the Sun, Saturn makes a journey of about 5.5 billion miles (8.9 billion km).

As each of the planets in the solar system orbits the Sun, it also spins on its **axis**. To make one full spin, or rotation, takes Earth 24 hours. Saturn is a fast-spinning planet, however, and it rotates much faster than Earth. Giant Saturn makes one full rotation in less than half the time Earth does, so a day on Saturn lasts just under 11 hours.

That's Out of This World!

If you could drive a car at 60 miles per hour (97 km/h), day and night without stopping, it would take just over two weeks to drive around Earth's **equator**. To drive around huge Saturn, however, would take about 22 weeks!

This image of Saturn was created from 126 photos captured in 2004 by NASA's *Cassini* spacecraft. Saturn has a diameter of over 75,000 miles (121,000 km).

SATURN, INSIDE AND OUT

Unlike Earth, Saturn does not have a solid outer surface. The planet is a huge ball of gases and liquids.

Saturn is made up of hydrogen and helium. These two gases are the same ingredients that make up our Sun and most other stars. Nearly 95 percent of the planet is made of gaseous or liquid hydrogen.

Surrounding Saturn is an **atmosphere** of ammonia, **water vapor**, small amounts of other gases, and ice. Winds in some parts of Saturn's upper atmosphere blow at about 1,000 miles per hour (1,600 km/h).

Beneath the planet's atmosphere is a layer of liquid hydrogen. Below this layer, and deeper into the planet, the liquid hydrogen actually becomes metallic, forming a layer of metallic liquid hydrogen. In the very center of Saturn, scientists believe there is probably a solid core. This core may be made of rock and ice, and is about the size of Earth.

That's Out of This World!

Huge, hurricane-like storms often develop on Saturn. They are known as Great White Spots. In December 2010, NASA'S *Cassini* spacecraft captured images of a hurricane-like storm on Saturn. In just a few weeks, the storm grew to cover an area of about 6,000 miles (9,600 km) by 11,000 miles (17,700 km).

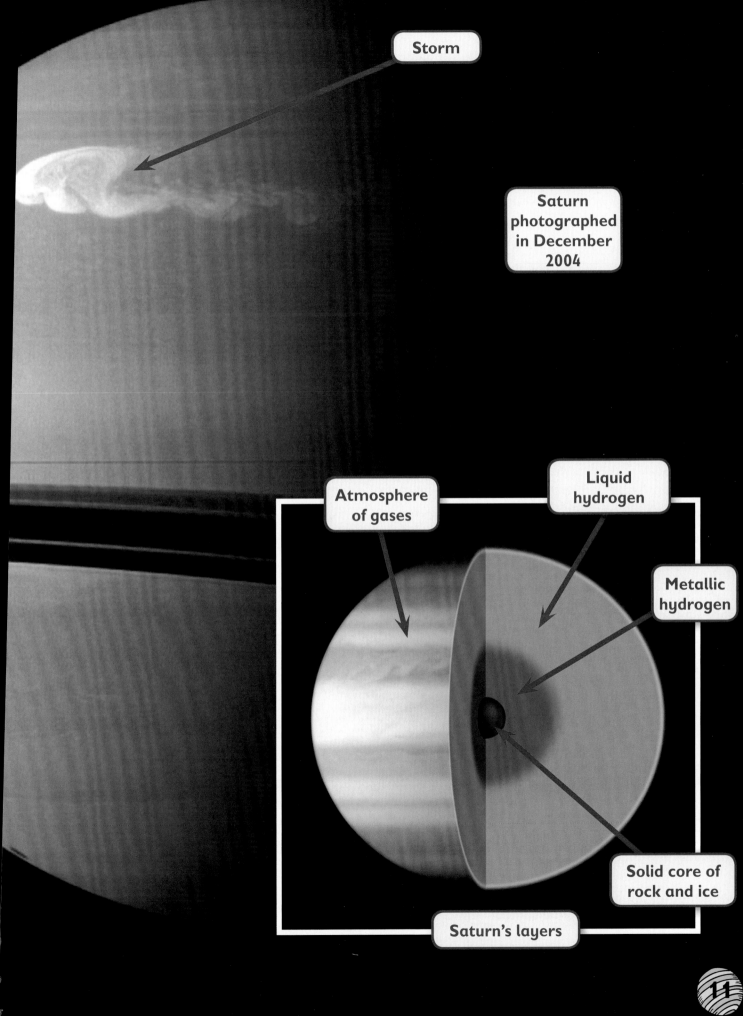

Storm

Saturn photographed in December 2004

Atmosphere of gases

Liquid hydrogen

Metallic hydrogen

Solid core of rock and ice

Saturn's layers

SATURN'S MYSTERIOUS RINGS

Ancient astronomers watched Saturn in the night sky for centuries. Then, in the early 1600s, the telescope was invented and astronomers could finally get a closer look at this distant planet.

In 1610, Italian astronomer Galileo Galilei was the first person to study Saturn through a telescope. Galileo saw objects on either side of Saturn. He drew these objects as other planets alongside Saturn, and later as arm or handle-like projections on the side of the planet. However, Galileo did not know what he was seeing.

Later, in 1659, a Dutch astronomer named Christiaan Huygens viewed Saturn through a more powerful telescope than the one used by Galileo. Huygens believed that what Galileo had observed was in fact a flat ring around the planet.

Today, with many decades of study through powerful telescopes and visits to the planet by spacecraft, we know that Saturn is indeed surrounded by rings that are made up of billions of particles of ice mixed with rocks and dust.

The Italian astronomer Galileo Galilei

That's Out of This World!

Some of the particles of ice, rock, and dust in Saturn's rings are as small as grains of sand, while others are as big as houses. A few are the size of mountains!

How early astronomers Galileo and Huygens would have loved to have seen this beautiful image of Saturn's rings.

SATURN'S ICY RINGS

Saturn's rings stretch into space from the planet for a distance of about 175,000 miles (282,000 km). The planet and its system of rings is so vast, that it would cover about three-quarters of the way from Earth to the Moon.

Saturn's rings of ice, rock, and dust particles are believed to have formed from pieces of **comets** and icy moons that traveled close to the giant planet. Before these space objects could get close to Saturn, however, they were torn apart by Saturn's gravity and pulled into orbit around the planet. As the chunks of ice and rock orbited Saturn, they collided with each other, breaking into smaller and smaller pieces to form dust and particles of all sizes.

Over millions and billions of years, these particles gathered to form the icy rings that encircle the planet, held in place by Saturn's gravitational pull.

That's Out of This World!

Saturn's rings are tens of thousands of miles (km) wide, but their average depth is only 33 feet (10 m).

This artwork shows how it might look to travel into the rings of ice and rock that surround Saturn. The planet is shown as yellowish-orange in the background.

NASA's spacecraft *Voyager 2* captured this image of Saturn's rings in 1981 during its mission to study Saturn and the solar system.

From A To G, Saturn's Amazing Rings

Saturn's rings are named with letters of the alphabet. It can be a little confusing, however, because they were named **A** to **G** in the order they were discovered, not in the order they encircle the planet.

This means that D is the ring closest to the planet, and the others then follow from the planet outward as C, B, A, F, G, and E.

Each of the rings orbits Saturn at a different speed, and they vary greatly in width. Ring F is the narrowest at less than 300 miles (500 km) wide. The widest ring, named ring E, stretches into space for about 186,000 miles (300,000 km).

The rings of ice, rock, and dust are separated by gaps, or divisions. The gaps also vary in width, from the narrow Kuiper Gap at just under 2 miles (3 km) wide, to the Cassini Division that separates rings B and A. This gap is 2,900 miles (4,700 km) wide.

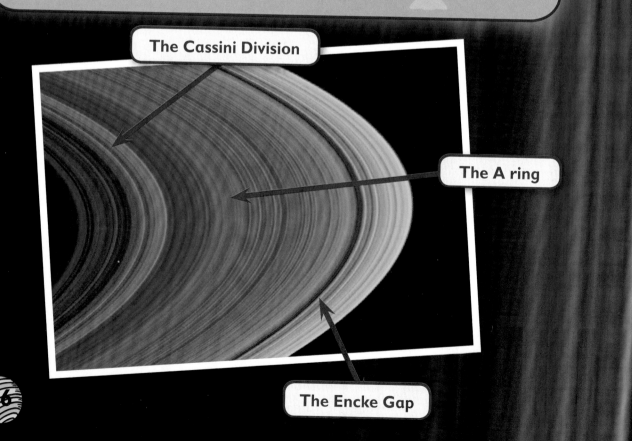

The Cassini Division

The A ring

The Encke Gap

This image shows from left to right parts of rings **C** and **B**. The greenish-blue areas are ice and the reddish-pink areas are ice mixed with dust.

That's Out of This World!

The gaps between Saturn's rings have been named for the astronomers who discovered them, or to honor famous astronomers from history. The Cassini Division was discovered by Italian astronomer Jean-Dominique Cassini in 1675.

SATURN'S MOONS

A moon is a rocky object that is permanently orbiting a planet. Mercury and Venus have no moons. Earth has just one, while Mars has two. All the other planets in the solar system have many moons. Saturn has at least 53!

Christiaan Huygens was the first person to discover a moon orbiting Saturn. He discovered Titan, the second-largest moon in the solar system in 1655. In the centuries that followed, Saturn's known moon count rose and rose. At the beginning of 2013, astronomers knew of 53 moons orbiting Saturn. There are other objects circling the planet, however, that might in the future be confirmed as moons, and there are possibly more moon-like objects to be discovered.

Saturn's moons have many different shapes and features. The moon Iapetus has a black side and a bright white side. Mimas has a huge **crater** where it was hit by an enormous space object that nearly split the moon apart.

The moon Dione

That's Out of This World!

Like a planet, a moon rotates on its axis. Saturn's moon Hyperion does not rotate smoothly, though. This may be because it's been hit by another space object, causing it to spin in a chaotic way.

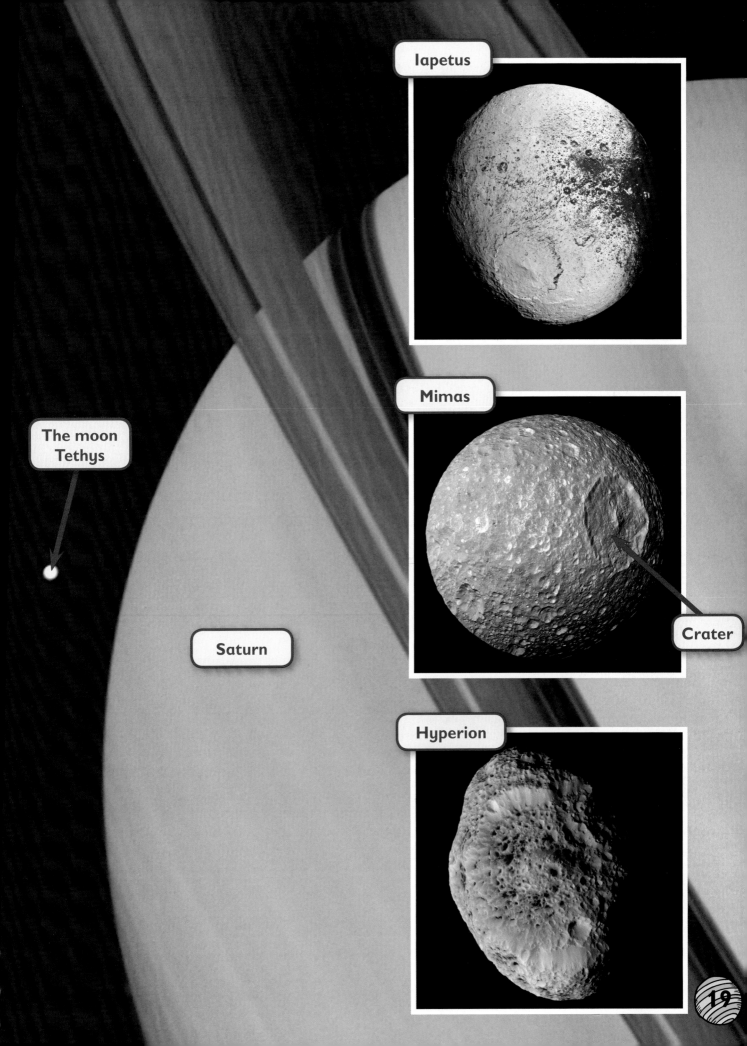

Iapetus

Mimas

Crater

The moon
Tethys

Saturn

Hyperion

19

CRATERS AND ICE VOLCANOES

Saturn's moon Phoebe is a round moon that is covered by craters created by collisions with other space objects.

Phoebe orbits Saturn in the opposite direction to most of the planet's other moons. Phoebe is made of very dark material. Scientists believe this moon originally came from the outer solar system where there is lots of darker material. As Phoebe traveled across the solar system it was captured by Saturn's enormous gravitational pull.

Enceladus is an ice-covered moon that has liquid water beneath its surface. This moon has many cryovolcanoes on its surface. Unlike volcanoes that shoot hot **lava** into the air, cryovolcanoes erupt jets of gas, ice particles, and even water.

Some of the ice particles that erupt from Enceladus's volcanoes become part of ring E around Saturn. In fact, it's believed that ring E formed from ice ejected from Enceladus.

This artwork shows a cryovolcano spurting ice into space from the icy surface of Enceladus.

That's Out of This World!

Some of Saturn's moons are known as "shepherd moons." These moons orbit in or near the planet's rings, and their gravity helps keep the particles in the rings held in place. Some of the gaps in the rings have been caused by moons that orbit inside the rings, clearing a gap or pathway.

Phoebe has a diameter of about 137 miles (220 km).

Enceladus has a diameter of about 313 miles (504 km).

21

TITAN

Titan, the first of Saturn's moons to be observed, is much larger than Earth's moon and is even larger than the planet Mercury. Titan has a diameter of 3,200 miles (5,150 km).

Unlike Saturn's other moons, Titan has been difficult to observe because it is hidden behind a thick atmosphere of gases that even today's high-powered telescopes cannot penetrate. Titan is the only moon in the solar system to have an atmosphere. Titan's atmosphere is mostly nitrogen with a small amount of methane. The layer of gases is about 370 miles (600 km) thick, which is 10 times the thickness of Earth's atmosphere.

Since July 2004, NASA's spacecraft *Cassini* has been orbiting Titan and studying the moon. Data from this mission shows that Titan probably has an outer layer of ice. Beneath the ice is an ocean of liquid water. Deeper into the moon there is more ice and a large rocky core.

Sun

Atmosphere

Layer of ice

Liquid water

Layer of ice

Earth's moon

Titan

Earth

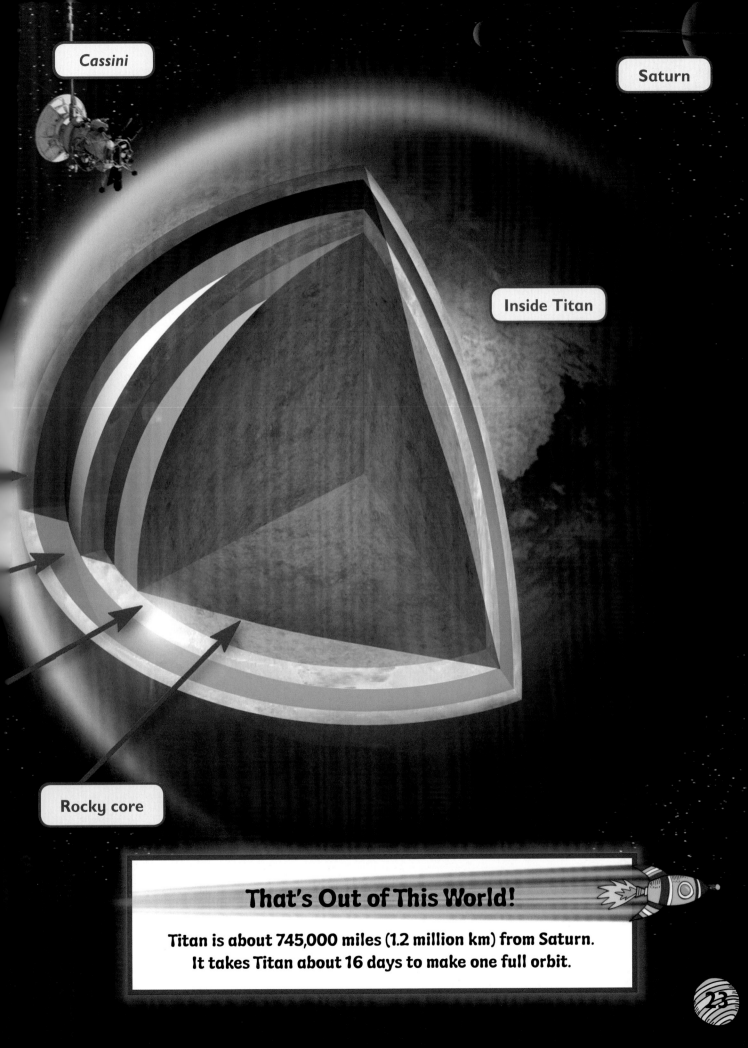

Cassini

Saturn

Inside Titan

Rocky core

That's Out of This World!

Titan is about 745,000 miles (1.2 million km) from Saturn.
It takes Titan about 16 days to make one full orbit.

MISSIONS TO SATURN

Astronomers studied Saturn, its rings, and its moons through telescopes for centuries. In April 1973, the first spacecraft to visit Saturn, NASA's *Pioneer 11*, left Earth on a mission to study Jupiter, Saturn, and the outer reaches of the solar system.

Pioneer 11 reached Saturn in September 1979. During its flyby of the planet, *Pioneer 11* discovered a new moon and the F ring, and collected data that showed Saturn is made mostly of hydrogen.

In November 1980, NASA's *Voyager 1* flew by Saturn. This spacecraft discovered Saturn's moons Prometheus, Pandora, and Atlas. Data gathered by *Voyager 1* also showed that Titan has a thick atmosphere made of nitrogen. Just under a year later, in August 1981, *Voyager 2* visited Saturn, giving astronomers back on Earth another chance to see Saturn, its moons, and its rings up close.

Today, *Voyager 1* and *Voyager 2* are still speeding through space. The spacecraft are traveling in different directions, but are both heading out of the solar system.

That's Out of This World!

In case the *Voyagers* ever encounter an alien civilization, each spacecraft carries a gold-plated copper disk containing information about humans and Earth. The equipment to play the disks, like records, is also aboard the *Voyagers*. Each disk includes 115 pictures, Earth sounds, pieces of music, and greetings in 60 languages.

The information disk carried by each *Voyager* spacecraft.

This image of Saturn and Titan (top left) was captured by *Pioneer 11*.

THE CASSINI-HUYGENS MISSION

In October 1997, NASA launched *Cassini*, the first spacecraft to orbit Saturn. *Cassini's* mission was to study Saturn and its moons.

Aboard *Cassini* was a car-sized landing craft called the *Huygens* probe. Named after Christiaan Huygens, the first person to observe Saturn's moon Titan, the probe was destined to land on Titan. Because *Huygens'* engineers did not know what lay beneath Titan's thick atmosphere, *Huygens* was designed to land on a hard surface or on water.

After nearly seven years of traveling across the solar system, *Cassini* entered Saturn's orbit in July 2004. To reach its orbiting position, *Cassini* had to fly through the gap between Saturn's F and G rings! Once in orbit, *Cassini* began collecting data.

On December 24, 2004, *Cassini* released the *Huygens* probe. When *Huygens* reached its destination, the surface of Titan, in January 2005, it would be the first spacecraft to land on any body in the outer solar system.

Huygens probe

That's Out of This World!

NASA, ESA (European Space Agency), and space experts from 17 countries worked together to make the *Cassini-Huygens* mission a success. Over 5,000 people were involved in the various stages of the mission!

Technicians work on *Cassini* before the launch. The spacecraft was named in honor of Jean-Dominique Cassini, the astronomer who discovered the widest gap in Saturn's rings.

Saturn

Cassini

This artwork shows *Cassini* releasing the *Huygens* probe on its mission to land on Titan.

Titan

CASSINI-HUYGENS AND THE FUTURE

Using parachutes to slow its descent onto Titan's surface, from 11,000 miles per hour (18,000 km/h) to just a few hundred miles per hour (km/h), the *Huygens* probe touched down on the surface of Titan on January 14, 2005.

As it descended through Titan's thick atmosphere, *Huygens* transmitted data back to *Cassini*. After landing, it continued to transmit information and images for nearly one and a half hours. Finally, scientists on Earth could see the previously hidden surface of Titan.

Since 2004, the orbiter *Cassini* has continued to send a daily stream of information back to Earth about Saturn and its moons. Today, *Cassini* is still in orbit, and its mission will continue until 2017. Among its many objectives, *Cassini* will look for evidence that the water on Saturn's icy moon Enceladus could be home to microscopic life forms!

Nearly 800 million miles (1.3 billion km) from Earth, Saturn still holds many secrets. Astronomers hope, however, that *Cassini* will continue to unravel the mysterious world of Saturn, the ringed wonder.

Images sent back to Earth by *Huygens* allowed an artist to create this view of the probe after its landing on Titan's surface.

Scientists were particularly interested in studying Titan because of its structure and atmosphere. Titan is similar to how Earth may have been in the time when life on Earth began. Studying Titan could reveal secrets about the history of our own planet.

This stunning view of Saturn was captured by *Cassini* in September 2006.

GLOSSARY

agriculture (AG-rih-kul-cher)
The science or practice of farming.

asteroids (AS-teh-roydz)
Rocky objects orbiting the Sun and ranging in size from a few feet (m) to hundreds of miles (km) in diameter.

astronomers (uh-STRAH-nuh-merz)
Scientists who specialize in the study of outer space.

atmosphere (AT-muh-sfeer)
The layer of gases surrounding a planet, moon, or star.

axis (AK-sus)
An imaginary line about which a body, such as a planet, rotates.

comets (KAH-mits)
An object orbiting the Sun consisting primarily of a nucleus, or center, of ice and dust and, when near the Sun, a "tail" of ice and dust particles pointing away from the Sun.

crater (KRAY-tur)
A hole or dent in the surface of a planet or moon, usually caused by an impact with another space object.

dwarf planets (DWHARF PLA-nets)
Objects in space that have certain characteristics that distinguish them from other bodies orbiting the Sun. One of these is that the object be large enough and its gravity be strong enough to have caused it to become nearly round. Also, its orbit around the Sun cannot have been swept clear of other bodies, as would be the case with the larger planets, and it must not be a moon of a larger planet.

equator (ih-KWAY-tur)
An imaginary line drawn around a planet that is an equal distance from the north and south poles.

gravity (GRA-vuh-tee)
The force that causes objects to be attracted toward Earth's center or toward other physical bodies in space, such as stars or planets.

lava (LA-vuh)
Rock that has been turned into a liquid or semiliquid by intense heat from within a planet, moon, or other planet-like object.

moons (MOONZ) A naturally occurring satellites of a planet.

nebula (NEH-byuh-luh)
A massive cloud of dust and gas in outer space. Many nebulae are formed by the collapse of stars, releasing matter that may, over millions or billions of years, clump together to form new stars.

orbits (OR-bits)
To circle in a curved path around another object.

planet (PLA-net)
An object in space that is of a certain size and that orbits, or circles, a star.

solar system (SOH-ler SIS-tem)
The Sun and everything that orbits around it, including asteroids, meteoroids, comets, and the planets and their moons.

star (STAR)
A body in space that produces its own heat and light through the release of nuclear energy created within its core. Earth's Sun is a star.

water vapor (WAH-tur VAY-pur)
The state of water, caused by evaporation, in which it ceases being a liquid and becomes a gas.

WEBSITES

For web resources related to the subject of this book, go to: www.windmillbooks.com/weblinks and select this book's title.

READ MORE

Allyn, Daisy. *Saturn: The Ringed Planet.* Our Solar System. New York: Gareth Stevens Leveled Readers, 2010.

Loewen, Nancy. *Ringed Giant: The Planet Saturn.* Amazing Science: Planets. Mankato, MN: Picture Window Books, 2008.

Sparrow, Giles. *Destination Saturn.* Destination Solar System. New York: PowerKids Press, 2009.

INDEX